CREATING A LEGACY OF YOUR LIFE EXPERIENCE AND WISDOM

THE GUIDE

By KARIN WEBER

ABOUT THE ILLUSTRATOR:

Renick's creative mind and exceptional artistic talent combined in a magical way to illustrate the points I wanted to make. Once again, it has been demonstrated that a picture is indeed worth a thousand words. He intentionally created line sketches so you can interact with them by adding details, doodles, or color.

Renick is currently "Artist in Residence" at Glenwood Springs, Colorado's Center for the Arts.

Here's his life philosophy:

"babies are born…people die…and, it is what we do in the middle that counts."

" i've known my share of problems, heartaches and disappointments because that is life – but i have also known a great deal of peace and joy that is the handmaiden of an inner freedom."

"i am not worried about what you think of me – but i do love you enough to be who i am and to let you know it is safe to be who you are –"

"the source of my energy is Spirit (being of service – what can i bring to the party – not what can i get)"

"i view the future 8 seconds at a time – life's a bull ride…"

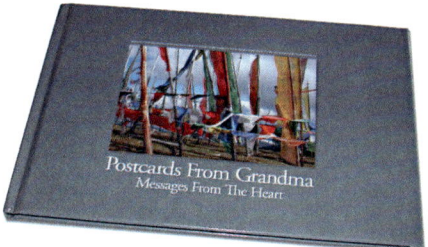

Postcards from Grandma, Messages from the Heart

The book inspired by this guide is available in selected bookstores, online bookstores and through the author at weberwrites.com

Copyright © 2007 by Karin Weber, M.Ed., M.A.
All rights reserved. No part of this publication may be reproduced, stored in a retrieval system, or transmitted, in any form or by any means, electronic, mechanical, photocopying, recorded or otherwise, without prior written permission of the copyright holder.

Printed in the United States of America
First printing August 2007

Creating A Legacy Of Your Life And Wisdom
ISBN: 978-0-9779930-1-7

To contact the author: grandmakarinweber@gmail.com, website: weberwrites.com

Unless otherwise credited, all photography courtesy of the author

Design and Production by McKenzie Designs, LLC

ACKNOWLEDGMENTS

This workbook is the synthesis of ideas and suggestions from many sources:
my great friend and mentor, Dr. Jane Healy, Ph.D.,
Craig White, my creative consultant and designer,
readers of <u>Postcards from Grandma, Messages from the Heart</u>,
and numerous friends who have talked with me about how to create their own
messages for posterity.

The underlying philosophy of both "Postcards" and this, its accompanying
workbook, is based upon the curriculum of the University of Santa Monica. I cannot
overstate my debt to Drs. Mary and Ron Hulnick for helping me to arrive at my truth
and to gain the confidence to speak it.

Last but not least, a huge "thank you" to the many friends who have read
this manuscript and offered their suggestions.

✱And His Mistake...was leaving the notes in the bottles Blank...

CREATING A LEGACY OF YOUR LIFE EXPERIENCE AND WISDOM: THE GUIDE

WELCOME!

The purpose of this book is to encourage and support you in identifying and documenting your personal "truth". It is my hope that after you have completed this "guide" book, you will not only better understand yourself, but also will have completed a keepsake and tangible representation of who you are and what you believe in.

The book is interactive: questions and exercises are presented in the hope of actively engaging you. I have selected a standard 8 1/2 " x 11" format so if you write with a laptop or computer, you will be able to staple or clip your writing within the book. Occasional comments describing my experience in writing my personal philosophy have been included in the hope that they will encourage you. These comments appear within gray-shaded boxes.

Work in any manner that suits you; I have formatted the book to serve not only as a guide, but also as a workbook. You'll find space to record information in the various lessons. Extra space has been incorporated so that you can jot down ideas that might not fit a particular lesson, but which you want to remember. There are also areas where you can sketch or doodle an idea or thought.

Now as you begin, rest assured that all that is required of you are sincere intentions
- to discover and document your wisdom

  and
- to engage in a willing suspension of disbelief in the process of getting out of your head and into your heart.

The payoff will astound you! I predict that in creating your legacy, you will experience personal enjoyment and enrichment.

So, let's get started!

*Or Look At Some Carrots And Say... "Crowd Noises And Rhubarb" ...Over And Over Again...An Old Oklahoma Meditation

EXERCISE ONE

WHAT IS IT THAT YOU WANT TO SAY? WAYS TO FIND OUT:

MEDITATION:

Find a quiet place where you won't be disturbed for at least 30 minutes.

Settle yourself into a comfortable position and close your eyes.

If it appeals to you, play restful music and light a candle.

Close your eyes and listen to your breathing.

Set an intention to be honest about your philosophy; do not worry what others will think.

Ask yourself:
- What is important to me?
- What can I tell others, both now and in the future, about my philosophy and what I know to be true?
- To whom do I want to speak? (i.e. who is my audience?)

Stay with it. As your mind wanders, listen to your breathing to refocus your thoughts.

Slowly open your eyes and return to the reality of your surroundings.

When you have identified key beliefs, write down or record what you have discovered.

> **My experience:** *I felt very self-conscious the first time I tried this. However, when I just relaxed and stopped judging meditation as silly, it became easy and effortless. Believe it or not, with time it has become natural and such an experience of comfort and insight that I have incorporated quiet times into my daily schedule. So if you are having trouble with meditation, don't be discouraged. Simply try again.*

However, if meditation just doesn't work for you, there are innumerable other means through which you can access your truth. Try listening to music, drawing, taking a walk, participating in a yoga or exercise class, napping – simply anything that quiets your mind.

DOODLES   NOTES

If you continue to have trouble with the discovery process, read through the following questions:

- What/who are/were the influences and influencers in my life?
- What do I wish someone had told me?
- What do I wish someone had NOT told me?
- What is my over-arching philosophy?
- What is MY truth? (Who am I and what am I about?)
- What have been my successes?
- What have been my "learning experiences"?
- What were some of the defining moments and experiences in my life? How have they shaped me and my philosophy?
- What has my life's journey been about?
- What have I learned that I wish to share?
- What is important to me, anyway?

If you're still having trouble identifying your philosophy, here's a thought-provoking exercise to try:

" I once heard this story about a priest who was confronted by a soldier while he was walking down a road in pre-revolutionary Russia. The soldier, aiming his rifle at the priest, commanded, 'What are you? Where are you going? Why are you going there?' Unfazed, the priest calmly replied, 'How much do they pay you?' Somewhat surprised, the soldier responded, 'Twenty-five kopecks a month.' The priest paused, and in a deeply thoughtful manner said, 'I have a proposal for you. I'll pay you fifty kopecks each month if you stop me here every day and challenge me to respond to those same three questions.'"

(Cashman, Kevin, <u>Leadership from the Inside Out</u>. (Provo, Utah: Executive Excellence Publications, 1998) 31.

If You Don't Know...You Are On Shaky Ground

How do YOU answer the soldier's three questions?

1. What or who am I?

2. Where am I going?

3. Why am I going there?

My experience: *This exercise truly helped me to get to the essence of what I deem important. Just challenging myself to answer the questions honestly led to a clarification of my belief system and to greater self-understanding.*

Use the following pages to record your thoughts.

DOODLES						NOTES

DOODLES

NOTES

DOODLES   NOTES

DO NOT EDIT YOUR WORDS AT THIS TIME!

Put your writing away and return to it in a day or two, amplifying or modifying it as necessary until it accurately reflects your philosophy and beliefs.

NEVER MODIFY OR EDIT YOUR WORK TO BECOME WHAT YOU THINK OTHERS MIGHT LIKE. THIS IS YOUR STORY AND YOUR WISDOM!

✳ What If I... (check any or all boxes),
☐ Offend Others? ☐ Lose Respect?
☐ Am Laughed at? ☐ Embarrass My Family?
☐ Don't Check Any of these Boxes?

EXERCISE TWO

ARE YOU BEING AUTHENTIC AND HONEST?

Now that you have discovered and recorded your message, test it by asking yourself if the words are coming from your head or your heart. A second test is to ask yourself if you are being "impeccable" with your words and truth (as suggested by Don Miguel Ruiz in his book, The Four Agreements).

"Being impeccable with your word is the correct use of your energy; it means to use your energy in the direction of truth and love for yourself. If you make an agreement with yourself to be impeccable with your word, just with that intention, the truth will manifest through you and clean all the emotional poison that exists within you. But making this agreement is difficult because we have learned to do precisely the opposite. We have learned to lie as a habit of our communication with others and more importantly with ourselves."
Ruiz, Don Miguel, The Four Agreements (San Rafael, CA. Amber-Allen Publishing, 1997) 33.

If you find that you are trying to impress your potential audience or viewer, you may need to revisit your intention to be authentic and honest. When you are finally satisfied with the honesty of your words, begin to organize your thoughts in a concise and comprehensible order.

> **My experience:** *This was a really difficult area for me since I had always been a gifted self-editor up until the time I wrote my book. What would people think? That question dates back to earliest childhood. What if I offended somebody? What if I lost respect? What if people laughed at me? What if I embarrassed my family? You get the drift of a noisy, judgmental brain! Finally, I got over it. And guess what? No catastrophe has yet befallen me. In fact, it feels really comfortable to have been open and honest.*

So, be honest with yourself. Use the next pages to refine your words and to make sure that they meet the tests of authenticity and impeccability.

_____
_____
_____

DOODLES   NOTES

DOODLES   NOTES

DOODLES   NOTES

EXERCISE THREE

WHAT IS YOUR MESSAGE?

Edit and modify your language to convey the ideas as powerfully and meaningfully as possible.

Repeat the editing process until you are satisfied with what you have written. This may take days or weeks, but stick with it.

If you are comfortable in doing so, ask a family member or friend to review your writing and tell you if they can easily follow and understand it.

REMEMBER! YOU ARE ASKING FOR THEIR ASSISTANCE IN HOW YOU ARE PRESENTING YOUR TRUTH, NOT FOR THEIR IDEAS ABOUT THE SUBSTANCE OF WHAT YOU ARE SAYING. THIS IS ABOUT YOUR MESSAGE, NOT THEIRS!

Are you surprised at what you're learning about yourself? To reiterate, this is not about what you want others to say about you, but rather what you want to tell them about yourself.

_____
_____
_____
_____
_____
_____
_____
_____
_____
_____
_____

DOODLES	NOTES

DOODLES					NOTES

EXERCISE FOUR

HOW DO YOU WANT TO SAY IT?

Now that you have successfully identified and clarified your message, the next step is to determine how best to present it. If you experience difficulty in deciding how to format it or which medium to use, refer to the checklist below for ideas:

- "History of Living" *
- Letters to family and friends **
- Photographs
- DVD's
- Music/CD's
- Visual arts (all media and types: oil, charcoal, sketches, cartoons, carvings, sculpture, quilts, design, photography)
- Journal, diary
- Photo essay
- Poetry
- Autobiography
- Oral history
- Genealogy
- Genogram *** (see "Resources" for information about John Bradshaw's <u>Family Secrets – the Path to Self-Acceptance and Reunion</u>)
- Family diary ****
- FutureMe.org. This new site allows you to write an e-mail to anybody and select the date for its delivery between now and December 31, 2037.

Some of these concepts may be unfamiliar to you, so in the next few pages I will explain them in more detail. And to give you a respite and/or inspiration, I've included favorite poems attributed to Ralph Waldo Emerson and Charles Harper Webb.

- * "History of Living" This concept is a scrapbook format pioneered by Drs. Mary and Ron Hulnick of the University of Santa Monica. It is a wonderful process which helps you identify and acknowledge those people who have been most important in your life.

DOODLES   NOTES

⏏ ** Letters to family and friends can span years and offer opportunities to thank special people for being part of your life (or maybe even to forgive them or yourself for past disagreements!).

Here is a sample letter from my own journal:

Dear Grandma, Thanks for having loved me. I remember that you were the only one who had time to help me build villages from Cherrios' boxes. Sometimes we took naps together on the couch. I told you my secrets – and I REALLY loved it when you told Mom to "…let it go; after all she is only a little girl."

I still find it amazing that despite the challenge of raising eight kids, you found time to organize the "20th Century Club" in the early 1900's. It's interesting to know that one thing you discussed was the "proper" role for women – should they teach or be wives and mothers?

I feel really privileged to be your descendant.

> **My experience:** *I've written letters to family and friends to express gratitude for how much they have enriched my life. The mere act of putting words on paper seemed therapeutic and forced me to concentrate on what was truly important. Describing my grandkids' unique characteristics and reminiscing about the special times we've shared was great fun!*

⏏ *** The genogram is a powerful tool for understanding family patterning. Just as genealogy deals with multiple generations, the genogram tracks family behaviors and attitudes across generations.

DOODLES   NOTES

> **My experience:** *I cannot overstate the value I found in completing my family's genogram. I questioned family members and friends to learn about my parents and grandparents. Some striking family attitudes and traits became immediately apparent during the process. On my mother's side, for example, the emphases on education and on being of service were paramount. On the flip side, I discovered a generational pattern of limiting self-perceptions. By recognizing the conditioning of my family's beliefs, I gained the opportunity to embrace or reject them (as opposed to merely accepting them as "reality").*

🔁 ****Multi-Generational Diary or Journal (multiple participants write daily entries which then are displayed side by side)

APRIL 19

Faye, (my mother) 1943: rain all day. Sleet at nite- about freezing. Washed today. Had to hang clothes in basement. Don't feel very good today. Starting on last month now. Hope it won't be that long, though.
Faye, 1944: beautiful day – 50 – 60- a little cool out of sunshine. Had Karen outside and took three snapshots of her.

Karin, 2007: C's birthday – 'can't believe she is 39! Did a bike ride to begin getting in shape for summer. There is that great hint of green in the aspens – impossible to explain but something I always love to see.

C (my daughter) 2007: a great birthday – the kids made cards and drew pictures for me. I went to exercise class and then we ate at Benihana's - R called from India to say "happy birthday."

R (my son) 2007: called C to wish her "happy birthday." Today it hit me: India is a truly special place - where else can you see 45 people traveling on a single tractor, all smiling despite their condition and just grateful to be alive? Flew back to Singapore and managed to get sleep as the seat next to me was open. Sometimes it's the little blessings that get us through!

A (my grand-daughter) 2007: - We all made a cake for Mommy.

The Great Mystery: Where Compassion Comes From...see...hear...feel...speak...

My experience: *My daughter, grand-daughter, and I are currently writing daily entries which we will juxtapose next to my mother's diary from 1943 and 44. Not only do my mother's words give me insight into how she thought and what she felt, but they also reveal what life was like during World War II. Because she died at a young age, we never knew one another as adults. Her diary has provided a really meaningful context through which to understand her and learn about her life as a young mother.*

In order to select the appropriate medinm, take time to return to the contemplative state described in Exercise One. Be sure that the format you choose is consistent not only with your intention to be authentic, but also that is well suited to your message.

Let your ideas flow uninhibitedly and freely as you work on the first draft; it can be perfected later. Now is the time to be creative.

When your draft seems honest, review it again and again. Now is the time to edit, clarify, enhance your work.

When you are satisfied with your efforts, check in with yourself once again to make certain that both the message and format are coming from your heart, not your head, or at least that they are a combination of the two.

My experience: *I discovered that by being contemplative, the format just popped into my head; I immediately recognized that it was right. What are you finding?*

DOODLES   NOTES

And now, the promised respite:

"Success Quote"
Attributed (probably inaccurately) to Ralph Waldo Emerson

To laugh often and love much.
To win the respect of intelligent persons and the affection of children.
To earn the appreciation of honest citizens and endure the betrayal of false friends.
To appreciate beauty.
To find the best in others; to give of one's self.
To leave the world a bit better; whether by a healthy child, a garden patch or a redeemed social condition.
To have played and laughed with enthusiasm and sung with exultation.
To know even one life has breathed easier because you have lived ...

This is to have succeeded.

How To Live
By Charles Harper Webb

Eat lots of steak and salmon and Thai curry and mu shu
pork and fresh green beans and baked potatoes
and fresh strawberries with vanilla ice cream.
Kick-box three days a week. Stay strong and lean.
Go fly-fishing every chance you get, with friends

who'll teach you secrets of the stream. Play guitar
in a rock band, read Dostoyevsky, Whitman, Kafka,
Shakespeare, Twain. Collect Uncle Scrooge comics.
See Peckinpah's Straw Dogs, and everything Monty Python made.
Love freely. Treat ex-partners as kindly

as you can. Wish them as well as you're able.
Snorkel with moray eels and yellow tangs. Watch
spinner dolphins earn their name as your pangah slam-
bams over glittering seas. Try not to lie; it sours
the soul. But being a patsy sours it too. If you cause

a car wreck, and aren't hurt, but someone is, apologize
silently. Learn from your mistake. Walk gratefully
away. Let your insurance handle it. Never drive drunk.

*Don't be a drunk, or and kind of "aholic." It's bad
English, and bad news. Don't berate yourself. If you lose*

*a game or prize you've earned, remember the winners
history forgets. Remember them if you do win. Enjoy
success. Have kids if you want and can afford them,
but don't make them your reason-to-be. Spare them that
misery. Take them to the beach. Mail order sea*

*monkeys once in your life. Give someone the full-on
ass-kicking he (or she) has earned. Keep a box turtle
in good health for twenty years. If you get sick, don't thrive
on suffering. There's nothing noble about pain. Die
if you need to, the best way you can. (You define best.)*

*Go to church if it helps you. Grow tomatoes to put store-
bought in perspective. Listen to Elvis and Bach. Unless
you're tone deaf, own Perlman's "Meditation from Thais."
Don't look for hidden meanings in a cardinal's song.
Don't think TV characters talk to you; that's crazy.*

*Don't be too sane. Work hard. Loaf easily. Have good
friends, and be good to them. Be immoderate
in moderation. Spend little time anesthetized. Dive
the Great Barrier Reef. Don't touch the coral. Watch
for sea snakes. Smile for the camera. Don't say "Cheese."*

DOODLES NOTES

EXERCISE FIVE

DETAILS, DETAILS.

Now the technical questions about production arise:
- Will you print or prepare multiple copies of your work?
- Are you able to complete the project on your own or will you need technical assistance from designers, printers, editors or others?
- If you plan to distribute your work commercially, what is your budget?

What technical information do you need to research in order to complete the project?

_____
_____
_____
_____
_____
_____
_____
_____
_____
_____
_____
_____
_____
_____

Where can you get help?
- Internet research
- Personal network
- Professional organizations
- Commercial assistance
- Other

Expect technical setbacks. View them as growth opportunities – annoying, yes – but inevitable. <u>What counts is not the issue of the setbacks, but rather how you deal with them.</u>

Facing the Issue ... Are You a Hammer... A Feather ... A River...

Do you now have all the technical resources needed to continue? You can use this page to list them and their contact information.

___

My experience: *This part of the project presented me with innumerable opportunities to work on myself! The entire exercise of producing a book afforded a huge learning curve. Who knew about pixels and fonts and TIFF? Not me, that's for sure! And I frequently was reminded that "the issue is not the issue. Rather, how one deals with the issue IS the issue."*

DOODLES   NOTES

EXERCISE SIX

BUT, WHEN WILL YOU FINISH?

For those of us who can't write nor sing a song, paint nor sculpt, our projects will probably require more work before they are completed. For us, it can help to break down the process into small, sequential tasks.

> **My experience:** By identifying a series of small steps, I was forced to concentrate on the process rather than the end-product. This made the project less daunting, more enjoyable and reinforced the importance of staying in the present moment.

TASKS	EXPECTED COMPLETION DATE	ACTUAL COMPLETION DATE

DOODLESNOTES

TASKS	EXPECTED COMPLETION DATE	ACTUAL COMPLETION DATE

My experience: *Boring as this goal-setting seemed, it really helped me to stay on task rather than to procrastinate or focus only on outcome.*

DOODLES   NOTES

EXERCISE SEVEN

WHO ARE THE BENEFICIARIES OF YOUR PROJECT?

Now that you have successfully completed your legacy project,

▶ What do you intend to do with it?

▶ To whom will you give it?

▶ Will you give it now or later?

✳ Lenick shares his Philosophy!

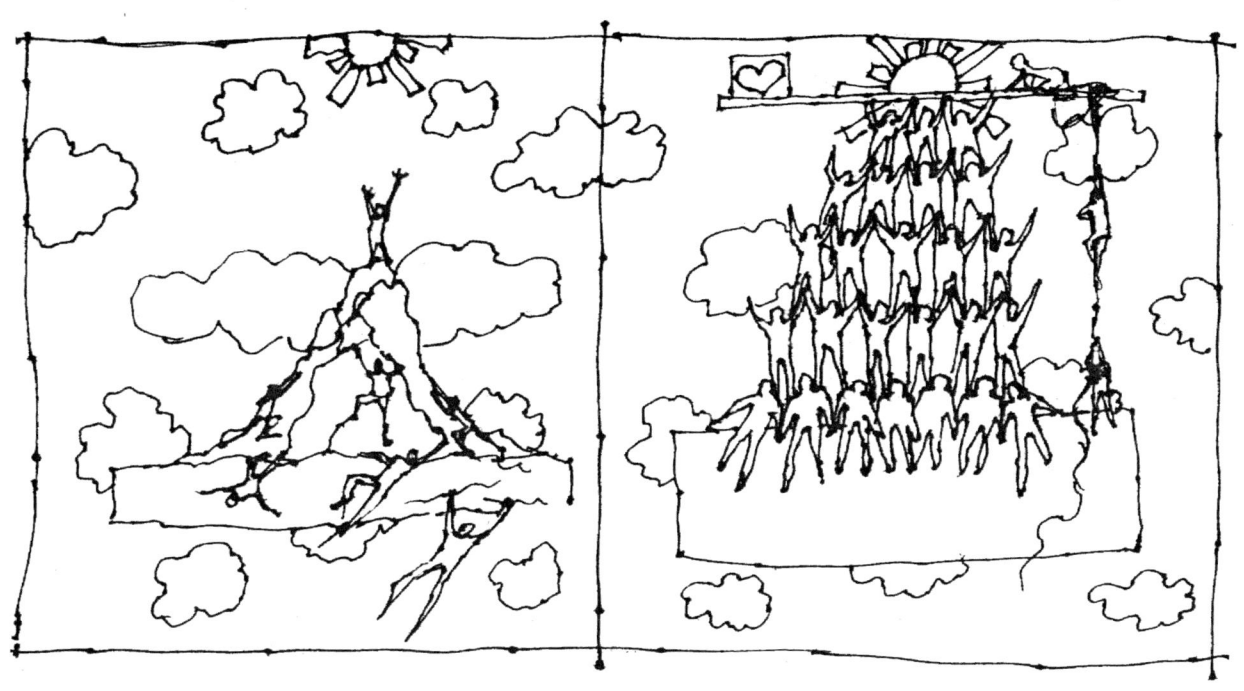

✳ Do You Wanna be Right ...or ...Do You Wanna be Successful...
You Alone can do It ...But... You can't do it Alone...

EXERCISE EIGHT

AND, SAVING THE BEST FOR THE LAST!

Congratulate yourself for having successfully compiled your wisdom and truth to benefit posterity!

What have you learned about yourself during the process?

Are you surprised at what you have discovered?

What obstacles did you overcome? How did you deal with them?

What emotional growth have you experienced?

RESOURCES

Bradshaw, John. <u>Family Secrets – the Path to Self-Acceptance and Reunion</u>. New York. Bantam Books, 1996. This book is an excellent resource for anyone who wants to better understand himself and his family's patterns. Bradshaw explains how to create a family map, commonly called a "genogram".

Cashin, Kevin. <u>Leadership from the Inside Out</u>. Provo, UT: Executive Excellence Publications, 1998.

Federation of Genealogical Societies (ww.fgs.org 512/336-2731)

National Genealogy Society (www.ngsgenealogy.org 800/473-0060)

Ruiz, Don Miguel. <u>The Four Agreements</u>. San Rafael, California. Amber-Allen Publishing, Inc, 1997. <u>The Four Agreements</u> is valuable for two reasons: it not only offers insight about universal traits, but also a unique philosophical approach to life.

www.shutterfly.com. This site offers the photographer creative formats to use in presenting his message.

Webb, Charles Harper. <u>Amplified Dog</u>. "How to Live". Los Angeles, CA, Red Hen Press. 2006.

Weber, Karin. <u>Postcards from Grandma, Messages from the Heart</u>. Edwards, Colorado. Weberwrites, 2006. The book which started Karin's odyssey.

Contact the Author at
grandmakarinweber@gmail.com
Website:
weberwrites@com